HOW to keep yourself safe in a CROWDED PLACE

Nikita Kaur

First Published in May 2023

ISBN: 978-93-93386-23-6

E-ISBN: 978-93-93386-10-6

BLUEROSE PUBLISHERS

www.BlueRoseONE.com

info@bluerosepublishers.com

+91 8882 898 898

Cover Design:

Yash

Typographic Design:

Hemlata

Distributed by: BlueRose, Amazon, Flipkart

How To Learn To Be Alone In A Crowded Gathering, Life Tech Us The Importance Of Living Alone When We Learn To Be Alone, Tow Thing Tech You To Be Alone Frist Is Your Responsibility And Second Your Work There Are Two Things That Can Never Be Thrown Off Our Shoulder Is Your Responsibility Your Work Everyone Run In A Race But Only One Get Price Similarly Many People Running To Get Seccuss But Success Come Those Who Have Put All There'strength For This Race.. What Is Your Strength Your Strength Is Your Responsibility And Second Is Your Work And Race Is Your Success.Of Life.Tow Things You At Any Cost From Both Your Shoulders Never Put It Down That Is Your Responsibility And Your Duty.Your Family And Your Job Life Tech Us Lot Of When We Learn To Be Alone..?. You Will Understand The Importance Of Your Life Then You Will Learn To Live Life Alone In A Crowded Gathering With Your Responsibility And Your Duties, There Is Only One Solution To All Your Problems Wow.To Learn To Live Your Life Alone In A Crowded Gathering. You Find A Wide Variety Of People In A Crowded Gathering You Will Also Meet .Good People In A Crowded Gathering People Party' Bad People Will Also Meet You Can Be Anybody, You Can Be A Singer You Can Be Actor U Can Be A Bejusness Man U Can Be House Wife.U Can Be Husband U Can Be Single Life Living Person U Can Be A Girl Or Boy U Can Be Political U Can Be Anybody Any Human Being Any Person,Wow To Learn To Live Your Life Alone In A Crowded

Gathering Let's See, We Know What If The Responsibility Are Too Big No Work Is Small Or Big In Anyone's Eyes, No Work Is Big Or Small You Can Make Everythings Beautiful With Your Responsibility In This Crowded Gathering, What Makes Us Responsible).,Its Your Mistake Makes Us A Responsible Person,L Et Me Tell You For Example You Your Self Gave Your Valuable Things In The Hand Of A Most Trustedfull Person On Whom You Trusted A Lot And, You You Told Him Teck Care Of This Thing Of Mine Till I Do Not Come.But That'person When You Come He Says That He Could Not Handle Your Item If He Gets Lost Then.You Will Tell Whose Fault Is That'person?No.The Fault Is Yours.Not That'person, Sitting With A Broken Heart And Blaming Others Won, T Help,.If You Learn To Take Your Responsibility By Being Alone In This Crowded Gathering Then Only You Will Be Able To Become A Responsible Person? Everyone Makes Mistakes In This Crowded World Whether He Is A Rich Person Or Poor Person? That'why Whenever You Have Made A Mistake In Your Life Then You Yourself Take The Forward Two Steps, Don't Take Two Steps Back, And Don't Look Down , But Up Your Eyes.... Because As Long As There's Is Breath, There' Is Hope). Because Your One Mistake Can Help You Make The Right Decision In Life Ahead?.Second Part.Crowded Gathering.Knowing The Difference Between Right And Wrong.Experiencing All Kinds Of Different Problems Of Others In Your Life.And In This Crowded Gathering,Among People ..In Your

Life.. Learning The Importance Of Being Alone. It Does Not Mean That You Sit In A Corner By Being Separated From Everyone.. You Have To Learn The Importance Of Loneliness In Your Life By Living In The Mix Of People.?How To Learn To Be Alone In A Crowded Gathering? What Is It That Forces You To Be Alone. (Tap) When Poverty Gets You Down? Then You Force Yourself To Be Alone) Or Then He Forces Himself To Be Alone. They Leave Their City And Find Work In Another Country. They Work Hard And Achieve Heights. You Can Be A Film Actor. .You Can Be A Singer. You Can Be A Writer. What Things Are Forcing Them To Forget What They Should Do For Their Better Tomorrow. Aya….The Answer Is That He Does Not Love Himself. ..He Doesn't Value His Life. He Doesn't Take His Life Seriously. A Small Problem Ends Their Life. ..When You Love Others More Than Yourself..If That Is The Case Then You Can Never Love Yourself..For Example Let Me Tell Yotheir Life Seriously..Those Who Are Not Taking Their Life Seriously They Don't Get Anything In The End. Dear Friends Try To Keep Yourself Strong In Every Situation And Try To Be Alone In Crowded Crowd:?Third Part. In This Crowded Gathering. Learn To Defend Your Honor. Some People Respect Others More Than Themselves. Let Me Tell You For Example. Some People Give More Respect To Other's Wife Than Their Own Wife. ,And Some People Work Under Their Boss, But Instead Of Giving More Respect To Their Own Boss, They Give More Respect To Other's Boss. Your Duty And Your Husband Or

Wife Is Your Respect And Your Honor. Some Children Respect Other's Parents More Than Their Own Parents. Pay Respect To Your Parents. Whether Parents Are Poor Or Rich, Do Not Be Greedy Towards Your Children And Try To Treat Them Well Because They Are The Hope Of Tomorrow's Future. Never Forget In The Crowd Of People That Your Work Is Your Duty And Your Family Is Your Respect And You Will Understand The Importance Of Your Life In A Crowded Gathering When You Will Learn To Live Your Life By Living Among People.?(4)Fourth Lesson. In The Midst Of A Crowded Gathering, We Have Come To Move Forward In Life By Doing Something Or The Other, Our Life Is Like That Of Businessmen, We All Have Come To Do Business. So Put Your Best Efforts In Whatever You Are Doing, Whether It Is A Small Task Or A Big Task You Are Doing, You Need To Focus On It So That You Can Achieve Your Goals?Fourth Lesson. In The Midst Of A Crowded Gathering, We Have Come To Move Forward In Life, In This Crowded Gathering. How Much In Some People's Lives.

Even if trouble comes, those people never stop living a wasteful life. There is a problem in your life, sometimes the relationship between husband and wife breaks. Sometimes someone's love remains incomplete. If you love someone more than yourself, then whatever may be the relationship, it will always remain incomplete, it will never be complete. It is equal to a dustbin..The relationship which remains incomplete is equal to a dustbin..So trust yourself 100% more than others. ,understand you! When there is a problem in your life, there is no problem to live with the garbage. Do problems come in your life to get out of the garbage life? From God., or that! From the side of the human who would want that your future is very good?, it can also happen in your life, time creates such a situation that your eyes become blind, caste, we do not understand the difference between right and wrong. get, Bad situations come in our life to get us out of the dustbin, to make our life better and better? Let me tell you for example. When you see a beggar on the way, first you bathe him! are dressed

Are, ,And ,feed him food, any one will show mercy to the beggar but here in our life's talk But till then blame Will apply until Don't shatter your mind by breaking it. Unless it weakens your strength? Until then snatch your identity. Take? Until it destroys you..Until it takes away everything from you.Increasing your problem?

Is Similarly in this crowded gathering how do we get our life out of the dustbin?

Even if there are problems, delete that too, (wearing clothes) new. Wear thoughts, new. Wear thoughts in your life like clothes, (food.word of mouth).keep yourself among good people, no man likes to keep himself among fools! Everyone likes to keep themselves among sensible people? Whenn pay attention to our clothes in a crowded gathering, then why can't we pay attention to our lives? You always keep your way of life clear and people who keep their way of life clear, the word has no meaning because they know what, for example I will tell you. When we go to the market. ,Then we see two...pass through the clean path.?.The garbage people! Don't pass by on the way! Who likes? In this crowded gathering., good person, bad person, rich person, poor person, everyone has to pass through the garbage road,..because it is neither the fault of any good person nor any other person. It is the fault of the 'bad' person, both of them are forced to pass through that path, in this crowded gathering, the path is visible to our life by giving importance to our life, we should always keep the path of our life clear,?दूसरे लोगों को अपने जीवन को टिश्यू पेपर की तरह इस्तेमाल न करने दें। Don't let other people use your life like tissue paper,

Let me tell you for example. Tissue paper is very soft, if you keep your life soft like tissue, then anyone will come into your life, play, use you and leave,That's why always keep yourself strict. Let me tell you for example. Tissue paper is very soft, if you keep your life soft like tissue then anyone will come into your life, play, use you and leave. ,That's why always keep

Rose lives among thorns, our life also lives among thorns. Our life is always in pain and suffering, sometimes on the top of the mountains, sometimes in the middle of the valley. Like a rose looks beautiful among thorns. A rose does not leave the company of thorns amidst thorns, in the same way, in this crowded gathering, we take care of any of our problems.? let your face shine? (7) ,How to know the power of the soul within us, how to recognize it within us,. So much power is hidden, Some people think they can get power through witchcraft, There is a power hidden inside us,,,,,No one can attract iron to itself. And neither can anyone pull iron towards itself, Nor can soil pull iron towards itself. Nor can gold pull iron towards itself. Neither silver can pull iron towards itself. Nor can soil pull iron towards itself. She can pull!..(magnet)shows your inner strength.,iron shows man's mind..iron shows man's thought also.iron also shows man's nature.magnet , shows a divine power. Iron cuts iron, the wicked end with the wicked, But you have to know that there is a divine power inside you, that is! The magnet, in this crowded gathering. inside us!don't use the magnet to please other person to attract other person to please other person.,,,,your inner power you have to use on their Whose thinking is heavy on you, ,Let me give you an example. You don't want to get married and your family members want you to get married. If, you would not have mixed yes in yes with their words,, So? Their thinking would not have dominated you. .,,, Now we pay attention to how their thinking dominated you Wanted to do. Right now u want to focus in your life, If you had told what is in your mind to your family members, then their thinking would not have dominated you.,, So? Their thinking would not have dominated you, Now you must have understood. In which place should we use our inner power?, In this crowded gathering.Some people's thinking is like iron.They have bad thinking which can never change your perspective.,,,Some people's thinking can be very wrong towards you, So where to put your inner power?Now days it is the era of social media.,We all are very active in social media.,You use your inner power here my .,People Try to understand and know the reason behind things., or behind the importance of words, ,,,, Good people are also found on social media. Bad people are also found.,,Good things and bad things are all on social media.,,, Try to understand and know the reason behind things.,,,? Behind people's words? What is the reason? Got that? And take care of yourself:?In this crowded gathering. In you can be present anywhere, anytime. Can be present in people, near the phone and on social media. Stay strong wherever you are but try to understand yourself and others as well. And caution yourself as well as others. Because social media is a huge platform. There are different platforms of social media but many people prefer to use Facebook, the reason behind this is? That people can make friends and talk to meets a bad person. (, Magnet. Shows the power inside us.), Many people make their lives. Many people waste their life. Many people make their life and many people's life is also ruined. Some people achieve the height. Some people lose themselves. That's why you are present anywhere in this crowded gathering. Try to understand yourself more than others. Try to know and understand deeply what is the reason and purpose behind them. Magnet shows your inner power,.Whenever you meet a stranger or? let's talk. By your inner strength. With your knowledge and your cleverness. The reason and purpose of his words. Try to know and understand. (2) If you do this, you will be able to save yourself as well as others from falling from the ditch.? The power to know the reason behind people's words?Sometimes it's better not to reveal yourself at all. Be a little revealing so people know who you are. You have the power to know the reason behind people's words, what in this crowded gathering, do you reveal to the people? You should not misunderstand my words and understand them well, so I am telling you by giving an example. (First point) you have such expensive expensive clothes?(Two point) so much? It is an expensive car. (3 point) Do you have such expensive house?, (4 point) Do you have so much money? Here you have to disclose your What art do you have? Everyone has different art. Some have the art of singing well. Some have the art of acting. Some have the mind to read, some have the art of writing. What is the secret behind all the arts? For the sake of caution and for the caution of other people, wherever you may be present, the person may be known or unknown to you ,, you must try to understand deeply the reason behind the words of their, mouth, with your inner powers.?,When you will get success in your life then how will you keep your attention on people,,,,,,,,

(1) To know the color of the rainbow mountain, we will pay attention to this point. These mountains of rainbow colors are present in western Peru and western China. Green, magenta, red and yellow mountains are present at this place, known as Zhangye Danxia Landscape. There are stripes of colors on these mountains in such a way that it looks like a painting to the beholders. Let's try to climb,,(3),The way the rainbow falls on the mountain.The color of all the mountains changes in different way,,,,in the same way we all try to get success in this crowded gathering. So everyone climbs on different colored mountains,,,,,, Different colored mountains show our work,,, When the rainbow falls on the mountain, the mountains turn into different colors. ,(,4,),Similarly when a person takes one step forward to achieve success.,So?He chooses a mountain of his own color according to his choice.,,To achieve success,one step towards success. It is not easy for anyone to grow, whether it is a mountain of any color.,, Whatever work it may be? It's not easy for anyone,,,,When you will get success in your life then how will you keep your focus on people,

(1) To know the color of the rainbow mountain, we will pay attention to this point. These mountains of rainbow colors are present in western Peru and western China. Green, magenta, red and yellow mountains are present at this place, known as Zhangye Danxia Landscape. There are stripes of colors on these mountains in such a way that it looks like a painting to the beholders. Let's try to climb,,(3),The way the rainbow falls on the mountain.The color of all the mountains changes in different way,,,,in the same way we all try to get success in this crowded gathering. So everyone climbs on different colored mountains,,,,,, Different colored falls on the mountain, the mountains turn into different colors. ,(,4,),Similarly when a person takes one step forward to achieve success.,So?He chooses a mountain of his own color according to his choice.,,To achieve success,one step towards success. It is not easy for anyone to grow, whether it is a mountain of any color.,, Whatever work it may be? It's not easy for anyone.,Every person moves forward to achieve success, they do not know that their

According to Laval, he will get the work done,,, but still he moves forward. Every person moves forward to achieve success, they do not know that their

According to the level, they will get the work done,,,but still,they move forward.Whatever color the work may be?,,,everyone works hard to get success, After getting themselves only in me, mine, mine, everything in themselves.,,, After getting success, those people become egoistic.,,,Some people get success in their life by choosing good colors,, It is not in the hands of some people to choose their own color as per their wish., ,,Goodness is breaking from inside me and I am slowly breaking down,,Goodness is eating me from inside.,,,My goodness has finished me. Can do. The inner goodness of a man is equal to the glass, breaking the glass is very

considered evil, in the same way as the intrinsic goodness of the human being. breaks down... then brings a lot of trouble to others,,,,,,,,,, @ ,When in this crowded of gathering. When (i and my word comes)then no relation can be seen except the self whether it is the relation or the property of our house,,, because the mind is full of itself,,, and when the mind is You fill up, our words go away from family, go away from husband and wife, go away from friends, and I and my words get absorbed in themselves,,,, me and my words Remove it from your life! It's going to be wonderful and if you use our word, it's a lovely word. Good to hear too. Because where my my my my my my my my my my my word comes. There is nothing to see except himself, he does not see anything except his things , he does not see anything except his worries. He doesn't see anything except money. except his family. They can't see anything. Removing his word!, When the word (mine) and (I) comes, that person does not think of any human being except himself., let's learn 8 part Flowers also have their own season. For example when season Of came it will be rising and shining also but when the reason is gone it will affect it will be affecting the flowers ALSO and when the flowers season came it will be growing and developing some new leaves on his body,Just as some flowers grow in rock, in the same way some flowers grow in water, and some flowers grow in stone. It is like a rock.,,,Mostly, these stones and rocks say a lot about how strong you are in life. When you are strong like a rock in your life, then in your life. Flowers will grow, flowers will bloom.,,,,,Let's go to water the flowers in the summer, fertilize the flowers to grow.,,,But God has created man to give.,,,,,,But when we humans wither. God has created a writer like us for you. Only then education becomes useful in our life. In ,,in a crowded gathering,,,we humans. Sometimes problems sometimes bad people Who is tidying up the flower? , , is sucking, who is sucking the flower, bee ,, bee prepares its food by sucking flowers. ,,, the life of us humans is like flowers and we human's word is like honey of bee Bee is small but works very hard to collect honey.,,,,, If we look at Honey then Honey eats her own children. Why?, Because there are some diseases in their children which., Bees have a lot of meaning.,,?Then we work hard like a bee,,,,,, No matter how many. how ups and downs our life is, but we should learn to work hard like a bee, if you are thinking of doing something big in life, but troubles are coming on top of problems, then you should learn to eat honey inside it . Needed crisis. ,(,Honey,. People's experience also shows. Man learns from his own experience and from other's experience, hey)

To achieve success by overcoming each problem, by eating each problem like honey, in the middle of each problem, like a bee eats flowers You also get the knowledge of.,,,,,, So you are eating honey instead of poison in every problem. ,,,,,,and when it comes to self defense,,,,learn to sting like a bee.,,,,for your own well being for your self defense for your family for others not to lose your identity people One has to protect others also.,,Where it comes to your rights.,,,Get up and fight your battle.,,,,, It is not an easy thing in our life to spread fragrance like flowers in every trouble. ,,But when it comes to self defense we cannot eat every problem like honey.,,,When it comes to self defense we have to learn to sticking??9 part In a crowded gathering, every person has someone or the other who helps him in times of trouble.

Those who have humanity There are two types of people who ask for help, first. The person who really needs help. (2) The person who

21

to fulfill your requirement. Have you forced yourself?
He extends his hand to you.,,,, If you have a grain of
humanity inside you,

22

You? Before helping the person in front, you should look at your inner eyes. open it first.,,,,,,then you will know that person from behind,,,good person knows that you have humanity in you that's why you are helping them.,,and bad person knows that That you are full of humanity inside you, that's why it takes advantage of your humanity. ,,, the person who helps you? it doesn't help you

That he doesn't have brain? That person has humanity inside that's why he helps you.,,,The person who has humanity is you.

that helps. Because there is humanity in him? Not because he doesn't have a brain?,,9 part In a crowded gathering, every person has someone or the other who helps him in times of trouble.

25

Those who have humanity There are two types of people who ask for help, first. The person who really needs help. (2) The person who

26

to fulfill your requirement. Have you forced yourself? He extends his hand to you.,,,, If you have a grain of humanity inside you,

You? Before helping the person in front, you should look at your inner eyes. open it first.,,,,,,then you will know that person from behind,,,good person knows that you have humanity in you that's why you are helping them.,,and bad person knows that That you are full of humanity inside you, that's why it takes advantage of your humanity. ,,, the person who helps you? it doesn't help you

That he doesn't have brain? That person has humanity inside that's why he helps you.,,,The person who has humanity is you.

29

that helps. Because there is humanity in him? Not because he doesn't have brain?,,,,, If you want that no one should take advantage of your humanity in this crowded gathering?,(,1,)You have to respect your humanity.,,, (2) Appreciating your humanity, and in this way you can keep your humanity alive.,??10. Wisdom doesn't come from studying more in life, when you stumble and suffer in life, then you get knowledge.? In a crowded gathering, some people study so much, study so much. study day and night,,, who are illiterate, we call them like this, they are not educated, they do not have knowledge,,, but it is not so, they are not educated. Can't write but can experience those who are much older than us. Those people have experienced life more than us. Wisdom does not come in life by studying more but by stumbling in life! sense,

Stumbling only makes you a wise person. Everything in the world breaks by stumbling. There is only one success which is attained by stumbling.? 10. Where. There is no respect for the relationship, there is no use by putting a price. where there is knowledge there are relationships

And where there is no knowledge, there is no fear of spoiling the relationship. And there is no use giving a good name to a bad relationship.?We give the most respect to. money. In this crowded gathering, many people even kill others for money and for some, money is nothing in their life. For some people, respect is a big deal. Money is not a big deal.,,,, We give utmost respect to our ID also because our identity is our image identity.,,.....When our highest respect increases on the person whom we called bad, when the problem in their life also comes in our life, then only we can understand the person in front,,,,,, then only we see The attitude of the person turns into respect for that person:?...Where. There is no respect for the relationship, there is no use by putting a price. where there is knowledge there are relationships

And where there is no knowledge, there is no fear of spoiling the relationship. And there is no use giving a good name to a bad relationship.?...There is no relation bigger than humanity. There is no religion bigger than humanity. There is no respect greater than humanity.? The biggest respect is for humanity.,,,,Where there is no humanity, there is no respect, where there is no humanity, there is no relationship, where there is no humanity, there is no religion.?Humanity is respected more than money.,,Always look up in this crowded gathering, how can we learn to always look up. Let's see on example we learn from elephant, elephant always looks up, it always makes noise with its mouth by lifting its nose up. Lion is the king of jungle but lion is also afraid of eion is also a victim of elephant! Becomes more than every other animal in the jungle. Humanity is found inside the elephant ? Some people may not help you but will definitely hurt you.?

the person who has humanity that person help others because he has humanity not because he doesn't have a brain. ,,,

They hurt you because they hate you.? ,,,,.

(1) your story is not my won story i am the seeker of my own story because everyone have there own life experience. (2). How to keep yourself safe in this crowded gathering , life teaches us many things when we learn to be alone and keep our self safe in this crowded gathering,...